The *Other*
Serenity Prayer

Meditations on Self-Kindness

Eleanor Brow**nn**

Heart Based Media
Los Angeles

Eleanor Brow**nn**

The *Other* Serenity Prayer: Meditations on Self-Kindness

First edition January 2023
Second printing March 2025

ISBN 979-8-218-11148-9 (print)

Published by Heart Based Media
Los Angeles, California, United States of America

Publisher Contact: www.heartbasedmedia.com
Author Contact: www.ebrownn.com

Cover image: Dawn breaking at sea between Australia and New Zealand on January 9, 2011. Photography by Eleanor Brownn.

Eleanor Brow**nn**

DEDICATION

May this book be a blessing to someone, somewhere.

MEMORIAM

In memory of Eugenie White.

Eleanor Brownn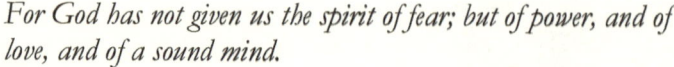

For God has not given us the spirit of fear; but of power, and of love, and of a sound mind.

2 Timonthy 1:7

Acknowledgements

I thank God, from whom all my blessings flow and who has given me so many second chances. Any success I have is God's, not mine. I thank my ancestors, known and unknown, related by blood and not related by blood, for loving me and protecting me on my life path.

Thank you to Lynette M. Smith of All My Best for editorial review, Aliye Çullu for technical assistance with self-publishing, Dr. Flora Brown for self-publishing consultation, and Carol Jenkins for Quality Assurance. Gratitude goes to the God Squad: Norman Beede, Chester Brown *(in memoriam)*, Eleanor Mae Daigre *(in memoriam)*, Margaret Gautier, Adela Guzmán, Linda Hurst, Lurecca Jefferson, Carol Jenkins, Judie Johnson, Leslie Lewis, Sandra Logan, J.V. Manning, Michele Moritz, Chris McNamara, Monica Plant, Robert Veze *(in memoriam)*, and my newly found relatives, the Haynes and Williams-Craig Families. And a very special thank you to the online community at Facebook.com/BrownnCares that has followed this writing journey since it began in January 2011; you held me up many times over the years when I was low.

Eleanor Brow**nn**

Table of Contents

Eleanor Brown**nn**

May you

be kinder

to yourself.

Eleanor Brow**nn**

Introduction

> *"God, grant me the serenity to stop beating myself up for not doing things perfectly, the courage to forgive myself because I'm working on doing better, and the wisdom to know that you already love me just the way I am."*
>
> — *Eleanor Brownn*

By January 2011, my life was upside down. A long history of perfectionism had finally caught up with me and brought me to my knees.

Perfectionism has nothing to do with achieving perfection. Perfectionism is the nagging belief that nothing you do will be good enough to measure up, so you either exhaust yourself trying to achieve the impossible or become paralyzed with the fear of making mistakes. It's that negative inner voice you use to beat yourself up for being human.

Perfectionism infiltrated every area of my life, including my personal relationships, my career ambitions, my finances, and my health. If I couldn't do it perfectly, why try? Or, if I did try, I'd endlessly berate the result (and myself) no matter how things turned out. The irony of trying to be perfect is that you become so afraid to make a mistake that your fear creates a self-fulfilling prophecy.

Eleanor Brownn

The breaking point for me came after a series of fear-based financial decisions that led to losing my home in Los Angeles, California to foreclosure just before the turn of 2011. I was devastated by the loss. On the cusp of turning 60 years old, never married, with no family, my home represented security in many deep ways – and now it was gone.

I couldn't stop beating myself up about it. Little did I realize my incredible journey of the heart had begun. I was alone, frightened, confused, and ashamed. I thought I was too old and "not enough" to begin again. I no longer had a home. My belongings in storage, I drifted.

My wandering took me to New Zealand, where I finally hit bottom. I found myself on Milford Sound looking at the totality of my life and believing I saw nothing but failure. I was financially, emotionally, and spiritually broken. I felt displaced, in every sense of the word.

But something incredible came into my heart as I looked out over the water of the Sound. With tears in my eyes, I heard a voice deep inside of me say, "I've made mistakes, but I am not damaged beyond repair. I'm okay. My whole life is ahead of me."

In that moment, my self-talk became rooted in a shaky faith that maybe God loves me just the way I am – mistakes and all. Maybe this was not the end, but a new beginning – a new beginning with a God who did not expect me to be perfect. A God who loved me especially

Eleanor Brow**nn**

because I *wasn't* perfect. I was the one who needed to be kinder to *myself.*

A few days later I began posting my personal reflections on inner-compassion one day at a time on a Facebook blog, while based in a hotel room in Melbourne, Australia. They were really love notes to myself, notes speaking the encouraging words I needed to hear from that voice that had told me I was going to be okay. My faith grew stronger every day.

As **Eleanor Brownn with 2 N's** I attracted readers from across the globe who followed because they felt the same self-doubt in their own lives that I did in this uncertain world. Sharing my inner love notes gave them a tiny ray of hope.

I continued sending out my tiny rays of hope daily over the passing years. As life continued to unfold, there were nights when I cried myself to sleep. But there were also mornings when I laughed myself silly. I gradually recognized that I was blessed beyond measure. There was prosperity and security in my life, even in the leanest of times.

I kept writing. I began to consider the possibility that what I saw as losses might actually be gifts in disguise. My housing stabilized over time, and I was grateful for my health as I continued on my healing journey as I approached age 70. Maybe I didn't need to be perfect. Maybe God really did already love me just the way I am.

Eleanor Brow**nn**

For 4,000 days since that January in 2011, no matter where I've slept the night before – from the bedroom suite of an ocean-view high-rise to the driver's seat of my subcompact car, or wherever the road of life has taken me in between – I have gotten up every morning and turned on my laptop to send a tiny ray of hope out into the world, sharing the healing lessons I'm learning about perfectionism, mistakes, and forgiveness.

In this handbook of poems, prayers, and positive self-talk, I offer a compilation of those tiny rays of hope.

May you be kinder to yourself.

*Eleanor Brow**nn***
January 1, 2023
Jefferson Park
Los Angeles, California

Hear the background story behind the cover:

Eleanor Brow**nn** 💬

How to Use This Book

Perfectionism – that inner nagging belief that nothing you do will be good enough – can stop you in your tracks and steal your dreams. How you talk to yourself matters. Beating yourself up doesn't work.

Eleanor Brownn began journaling the words she needed to hear to combat her own perfectionism while walking past her fears, challenges, and self-doubt with faith, hope, courage, and love. She shared those words with the world in a series of "inner love notes" across a decade on social media as *Eleanor Brownn with 2 N's* (facebook.com/brownncares).

With its one-life-lesson-at-a-time format, *The Other Serenity Prayer: Meditations on Self-Kindness* contains her heart-based poems, reflections, and gentle inspirations to take a break from the negative voice inside our heads.

Her love notes are divided into eight themes: Inner-Compassion, Healing, Believing, Mindfulness, Making Space for God, Respecting the Journey, Lifelong Learning, and Gratitude.

It's the type of book you can open at any page to give yourself a quick reminder to ***watch your words; your heart is listening.***

Eleanor Brown**nn**

Poems,

Prayers,

& Positive

Self-Talk

Inner-Compassion

Eleanor Brownn

God,

grant me the serenity

to stop beating myself up

for not doing things perfectly,

the courage to forgive myself

because I'm working

on doing better,

and the wisdom to know

that you already love me ...

just the way I am.

Inner-Compassion

Eleanor Brown**nn**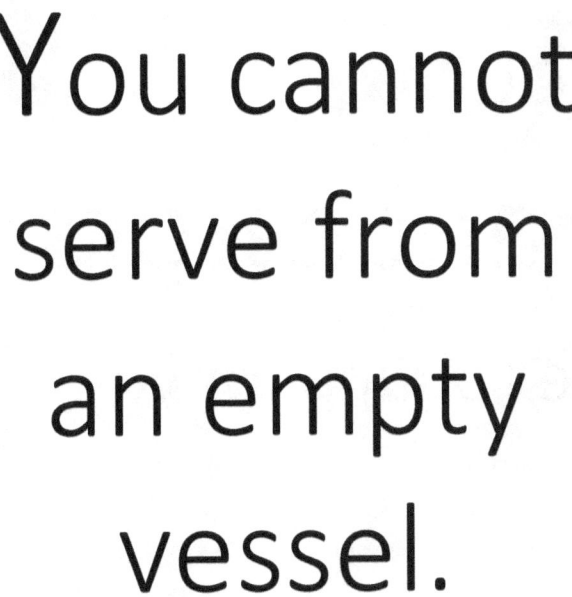

You cannot serve from an empty vessel.

Inner-Compassion

Eleanor Brow**nn** 🫧

Your

ancestors

are rooting for you.

Inner-Compassion

Eleanor Brown**nn**

Always

be kinder
to yourself

whenever you're going through a

difficult situation. Get more rest,

eat better food, and don't beat

yourself up for not handling things

perfectly.

Inner-Compassion

Eleanor Brownn

Staying positive

doesn't mean ignoring reality.

It means taking care of yourself so you can face whatever challenge is in front of you.

Stop, rest, and redirect your thoughts in a positive direction.

Inner-Compassion

Eleanor Brow**nn**

Time will pass,

things will change, and

you will make it through.

Inner-Compassion

Eleanor Brownn

Even small things can make a difference . . . a cup of tea, a quiet thought, or looking up at the sky.

Today, take a few moments to be a little bit kinder to yourself.

Inner-Compassion

Eleanor Brow**nn**

Be gentle.

Change takes time.

Inner-Compassion

Eleanor Brownn 💟

If you knew then what you know now, you would have handled things differently.

But you didn't know then what you know now, so you did the best you could.

Inner-Compassion

Eleanor Brow**nn**

Everyone makes **mistakes.**

Don't beat yourself up for being human.

And don't let anybody else beat you up for it either.

Eleanor Brow**nn**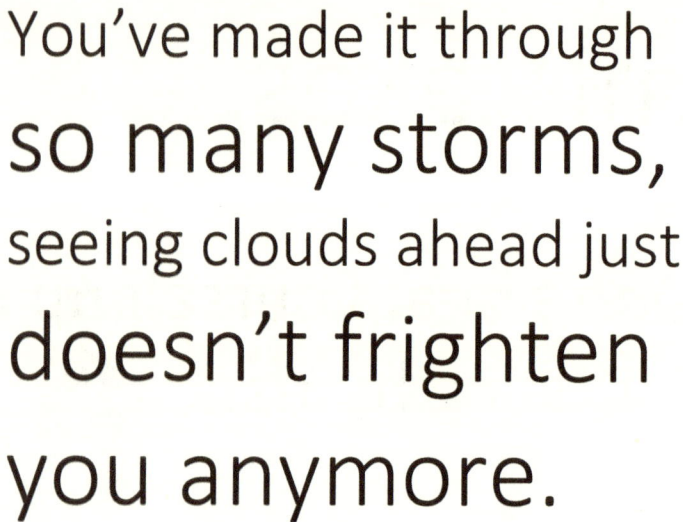

You've made it through
so many storms,
seeing clouds ahead just
doesn't frighten
you anymore.

Eleanor Brown**nn**

STOP

punishing yourself
for what
somebody else did.

Inner-Compassion

Eleanor Brow**nn** 💬

May you find yourself surrounded by

love

because everyone needs a day like that.

Inner-Compassion

Eleanor Brown**nn**

It's easier to

look through a

magnifying glass than to

look into a mirror.

But you'll learn more
from the mirror.

Inner-Compassion

Eleanor Brownn

There's a certain kind of peace that comes from accepting the cards you've been dealt and playing them the best that you can.

Eleanor Brow**nn** 💬

Real change takes small, consistent acts of courage. Give yourself credit even if you only make just a baby step today, because baby steps can be...

the hardest ones...

to take.

Inner-Compassion

Eleanor Brow**nn**

Have fun and be kinder to yourself.

Inner-Compassion

Eleanor Brown**nn**

Every single thing created
has its own special light.
No two are the same.

So it is as well with us
human beings.

Everyone has something
special to bring to the world.

Everyone.

Including you.

Inner-Compassion

Eleanor Brow**nn** 💬

Just shine.

You have no control where the light goes.

Let the universe decide.

Eleanor Brownn 💬

The world really isn't a very big place.

The air you breathe, the water you drink, and the earth you stand on are connected to all other people on all other parts of the globe.

Peace.

Inner-Compassion

Eleanor Brow**nn**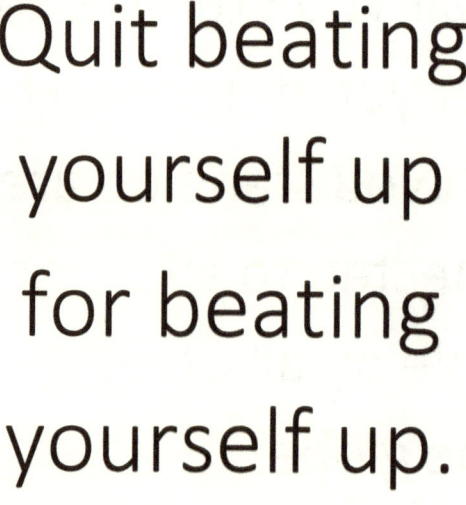

Quit beating yourself up for beating yourself up.

Inner-Compassion

Eleanor Brow**nn** 💬

Be wary of anyone who tries to convince you that **self-care** is somehow wrong.

Every living thing needs periods of rest in order to remain healthy.

There's nothing noble about running yourself into the ground.

Inner-Compassion

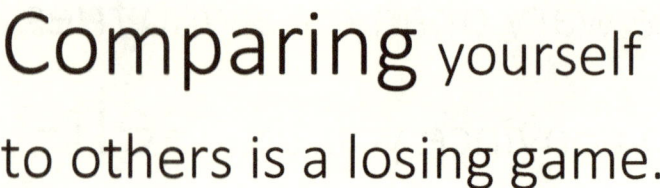

Comparing yourself to others is a losing game.

Do the inner work to develop your potential, because God gave you a special spark that's all your own.

Eleanor Brown**nn**

Maybe it's not a loss.

Maybe it's what

needed to be removed

so ultimately you can

be everything you're

meant to be.

Inner-Compassion

Eleanor Brownn

Quite often, the only peace to be made

is the peace you finally make

within yourself.

Eleanor Brow**nn**

Be the beautiful
soul you were created
to be and just shine.

The world can always
use a little more light.

Eleanor Brow**nn**

Pause-itivity

(the power of pausing).

Before you react, stop, think, and consider your options.

Eleanor Brow**nn**

Don't think too much.
It's bad for your health.

Inner-Compassion

Eleanor Brownn

Your mind may not understand how all of the pieces fit together,

but your heart does.

Inner-Compassion

Eleanor Brown**nn**

May a gentle
peace be yours
throughout
this day.

Inner-Compassion

Eleanor Brownn

Some questions don't

have answers, no

matter how much your

heart wants them to.

Inner-Compassion

Eleanor Brow**nn**

Sometimes you have to say

"no"

to people who don't want to hear it.

Setting realistic boundaries takes courage and practice.

Eleanor Brownn

Ultimately,
life is about
making peace
with your choices.

Inner-Compassion

Eleanor Brow**nn**

Only you know where the journey began and how very far you have come.

Inner-Compassion

Eleanor Brow**nn**

Mistakes?

Relax. You don't have enough power to mess up God's plan.

Healing

Eleanor Brownn

Rest and self-care are so important.

When you take time to
replenish your spirit,
it allows you to serve others
from the overflow.

You cannot serve from
an empty vessel.

Healing

Eleanor Brow**nn**

Some people
won't love you,
no matter what
you do.

Some people
won't ***stop*** loving you,
no matter what
you do.

Go where the love is.

Healing

Eleanor Brownn

You thought it would

break you in two,

but it made you

twice as strong.

Eleanor Brow**nn**

If God
took a selfie,
it would
look like you.

Healing

Eleanor Brownn

Sunflowers always turn in the direction of light because they instinctively know it's a source of strength and renewal.

Take a lesson from the sunflower. Look for the light in your world.

Eleanor Brown**nn** 💟

You're not the type
to give up hope.

You've seen too many
miracles happen...

...when it seemed all
hope was lost.

Healing

Eleanor Brownn

A **comeback** is a

setback that did its

homework, learned the lesson,

and then moved forward.

Healing

Eleanor Brow**nn**

Take time to nurture your soul.

Healing

Eleanor Brownn

Self-care

is any action you purposefully take to improve your physical, emotional, or spiritual wellbeing — getting more rest, eating healthier food, spending more time in thoughtful reflection, being kinder to yourself, smiling more, playing, or engaging in any activity that renews you.

Healing

Eleanor Brow**nn**

Write a new story
with every breath.

Healing

Eleanor Brownn

Be too busy living to have time to worry about what other people think.

Healing

Eleanor Brow**nn**

You had to smile the day you woke up and realized that the very thing you thought you couldn't live without was exactly what you needed to get rid of.

Healing

Eleanor Brownn

You are more
than a survivor.

You have been
transformed.

Healing

Eleanor Brow**nn**

Most life

lessons must

be learned

more than once.

Healing

Eleanor Brownn

Say goodbye to yesterday.

It won't be coming back.

Healing

Eleanor Brow**nn**

Take good
care of yourself.

Without your
health, very little
else matters.

Healing

Eleanor Brownn

You can become discouraged by the words

of your critics

or emboldened by the words of your

cheerleaders.

You get to choose where to focus your attention.

Healing

Eleanor Brow**nn**

Words have power,

but the only power

they have is

the power

you give them.

Healing

Eleanor Brownn

Upon quiet reflection, in spite of it all, there's been a lot of good in your life – more good than many others have seen, and more good than you could ever have hoped for.

Healing

Eleanor Brow**nn**

Be patient, because *you will be okay.*

Yes, it hurts right now.
But you are learning lessons
you can learn no other way.
You will emerge from the
darkness with a renewed
spirit and a deeper
understanding of who you
are and how strong you are.

Have faith. Hold on. *You will be okay.*

Healing

Eleanor Brownn

If you've always been a

people-pleaser and

you decide to stop

pleasing people,

please be prepared that

people will probably

not be pleased.

Healing

Eleanor Brow**nn**

May you stand strong and recognize your beauty, strength, and power.

Healing

Eleanor Brownn

Miracles often come in disguise.

What seems a hurtful situation may prove to be the very thing that propels you into a new and better direction.

Believing

Eleanor Brownn

Just breathe.

You don't have to figure it all out today.

Believing

Eleanor Brownn

Don't give up before the miracle.

That blessing with your name on it may be a whole lot closer than you think.

Believing

Eleanor Brownn

Sometimes, life brings you something that's just too hard for your heart to handle.

It can make you question everything you thought you knew.

And all you can do is take one moment at a time and hold on.

Believing

Eleanor Brow**nn** ♥

Don't set **your** sights low, just because **someone else** has a limited view of life's possibilities.

One person' s **comfort zone** might be another person's **cage.**

Believing

Eleanor Brow**nn**

L et Time be Time,

and let God be God.

Believing

Eleanor Brow**nn**

Plant your garden

with the things

you want to see grow.

Believing

Eleanor Brownn

It doesn't have to be perfect.

Just take it one blessed day,
one blessed step,
one blessed breath,
at a time.

Believing

Eleanor Brown**nn**

Walk in confidence today, knowing that

God is bigger

than any problem that may cross your path.

Believing

May you and all those you hold dear remain healthy, strong, and safe in a circle of loving peace.

Eleanor Brow**nn**

K

eep your mind on what supports your wellbeing.

Focus on what nurtures you, on what gives you strength.

Believing

Eleanor Brow**nn**

Faith or

fear?

You get to choose where to place your attention.

Believing

Eleanor Brow**nn**

The only thing on Earth you can count on is that there is nothing on Earth you can count on.

Believing

Eleanor Brown**nn**

If you believe someone else has to change before you can be happy, you will never be happy.

Eleanor Brow**nn**

Have quiet *faith.*

Nothing can rob you of your joy unless you allow it to.

Believing

Eleanor Brow**nn**

Plant your
tiny seeds.

Do not worry
whether or not
they take root.

Eleanor Brown**nn**

Keep some space in your tender heart for just a little bit of magic to happen.

Believing

Eleanor Brow**nn**

In the midst of the storm, may a

peaceful

heart

be yours.

Believing

Eleanor Brow**nn**

May you

grow stronger

with every breath

you take.

Believing

Eleanor Brownn

If something isn't working, doing more of it probably isn't the solution.

Believing

Eleanor Brow**nn**

Either you

believe

there's a plan

or you don't.

Believing

Eleanor Brown**nn**

Your

freedom

doesn't have to look like anybody else's.

Believing

Mindfulness

Eleanor Brownn

Always take time to listen to your heart. Your inner GPS will tell you when you've drifted off course.

Mindfulness

Eleanor Brow**nn** 💬

You used to say it was okay,
even when it really wasn't
okay, because you didn't
want to rock the boat.

But the price for that
became too high.

Mindfulness

Eleanor Brownn 💬

Be on the lookout for angels who cross your path today.

And you never know . . . you might turn out to be someone else's angel.

Mindfulness

Eleanor Brownn

There is **a part deep within you** *that is* complete and God-given. It was complete the day you were born.

No matter what time gives or takes away, remember to love and treasure that part of who you are.

Mindfulness

Eleanor Brownn

Quietly, gently, pay attention to what your heart is telling you.

So often it has an answer, if only you will take the time to listen.

Eleanor Brown**nn**

It's not about
the way things turn out.

It's about how you handle
the way things turn out.

You get to write

that script.

Mindfulness

Eleanor Brownn

Pay attention to what you're doing.

Mindfulness

Eleanor Brow**nn**

Always know
your worth.

Always shine
your light.

Mindfulness

Eleanor Brown**n**

Pursuing your dreams means listening to your heart and taking chances.

Yes, even when you're really scared to do it.

Mindfulness

Eleanor Brow**nn**

Watch your words.

Your heart is listening.

Mindfulness

Eleanor Brownn

Follow your vision, even if others can't see it.

Your dreams were put in your heart for a reason.

Eleanor Brow**nn**

It took a very long time for you to accept you could not go back there.

It took an even longer time for you to realize you don't want to.

Mindfulness

Eleanor Brownn

When you listen to your heart and recognize what it is you really want, only then can you find the courage to ask for it.

Eleanor Brown**nn**

Outside appearances can be deceptive.

The true value of something can only be calculated from within your heart.

Mindfulness

Eleanor Brown**nn**

When life gives you a
wake-up call,
you can either get up or roll over and go back to sleep.

Your choice.

Think about it.

Mindfulness

Making Space
for God

Eleanor Brown**nn**

Clutter is not just physical stuff.

It's old ideas,
toxic relationships,
and bad habits.

Clutter is anything that does not support your better self.

Eleanor Brow**nn** 💬

Letting go

may sound so simple,
but rarely is it a
one-time thing.

Just keep letting go,

until one day it's gone

for good.

Eleanor Brow**nn**

Sometimes when you lose something, you realize you never needed it in the first place.

Eleanor Brow**nn**

Clearing away clutter
is good for the soul
because it allows your
surroundings to be a
reflection of the person
you are today –
not the person you
were yesterday.

Making Space for God

Eleanor Brownn

Look within.

You may already possess the very thing you're searching for.

Eleanor Brown**nn**

When you hold on to something because you're afraid to let it go, there's no way for something better to enter your life. Whether it's a situation, an object, or an idea, if it doesn't support your wellbeing, release it.

Make space for God.

Making Space for God

Eleanor Brow**nn**

Let go of the things that do not reflect who you are now.

Making Space for God

Eleanor Brow**nn**

Declutter your heart.

Focus your time, love, and attention on people, activities, and things that deepen your spirit rather than deplete it.

Making Space for God

Eleanor Brow**nn**

There will never be
"enough" until you
realize you had it all
the day you were born.

Eleanor Brownn

Physical clutter can be a way to hide what you don't want to face – unfulfilled dreams, broken promises, or painful experiences from the past. Be gentle with yourself when you declutter. As you handle each item, quietly say a prayer, let it go, then move on. Trust that if you need the item, it will come back to you in another form at the proper time.

Making Space for God

Eleanor Brow**nn**

We came with nothing.

We leave with nothing.

Everything is temporary.

Enjoy the sunlight
while you have it.

It's good to be alive.

Making Space for God

Eleanor Brownn

When you reach the end of the journey, you probably won't be thinking about the clothes you wore, the car you drove, or the money you made.

You'll remember the love you shared, the adventures you had, and the people you met along the way – the people you helped and the people who helped you.

So try not to worry so much about material things. They will pass.

Love is what lives on.

Making Space for God

Eleanor Brow**nn**

Everything you need is already rooted in your soul.

Making Space for God

Respecting
the Journey

Eleanor Brow**nn**

STOP thinking you're
doing it all wrong.

Your path
doesn't look like
anybody else's
because
it can't,
it shouldn't,
and it won't.

Eleanor Brow**nn**

Maybe that roadblock you seem to keep coming up against is actually protecting you from being in the wrong place at the wrong time.

Respecting the Journey

Eleanor Brownn

Feeling lost and confused sometimes is just part of being on a journey.

Be patient with yourself.

No one is sure-footed every step of the way.

Respecting the Journey

Eleanor Brow**nn**

May your journey be filled with peace, happiness, and (most of all) Love.

Start from
your heart.

The greatest
journeys begin
on the inside.

Eleanor Brow**nn**

You don't have to wait until you get to **the top** of a mountain to enjoy the view.

Eleanor Brow**nn**

A baby step is still a step.

Respecting the Journey

Eleanor Brow**nn**

Haters gonna hate.
Underestimaters
gonna underestimate.

Keep moving forward.

Respecting the Journey

Eleanor Brownn

If you keep waiting until everything is perfect, you'll never get started.

And if you keep going until everything is perfect, you'll never get finished.

Respecting the Journey

Eleanor Brown**nn**

Life is a never-ending journey of self-discovery.

Learning who you are, what you like, what you don't, and what you want to do is a natural part of being alive. And it changes over time. Who you are today is not who you were yesterday, and it's not who you will be tomorrow.

Don't judge yourself for not having it all figured out.

Just enjoy the ride.

Respecting the Journey

Eleanor Brown**nn**

If you really stop and
think about it, your
Comfort Zone
probably isn't all
that comfortable.

Respecting the Journey

Eleanor Brownn

Starting over isn't really "starting over" because you're not the same person you were the last time you started.

What it really means is that you are taking lessons you've learned and applying them to the next phase of your life.

You're not starting over, you're moving forward.

Respecting the Journey

Eleanor Brown**n**

You've **climbed**
too many mountains,
and **crossed**
too many rivers,
to stop and turn
back now.

Respecting the Journey

Eleanor Brow**nn**

Every journey
has its own
special beauty.

Look for the
beauty in yours.

Respecting the Journey

Eleanor Brown**n**

The best way to reach your destination is to just keep going until you get there.

Eleanor Brow**nn**

It can be hard to hold
on to your vision
because other people will

want you to be like they are.

But your life has a course of

its own, and only you
can walk it.

Respecting the Journey

Eleanor Brownn

The amazing thing about a long journey is that you can miss exits, run STOP signs, head the wrong way down a one-way street, get lost, backtrack, and still, somehow, miraculously reach your proper destination.

Eleanor Brownn

Someone you meet along

the way today will need a

little extra bit of

kindness.

Travel with a gentle heart.

Respecting the Journey

Eleanor Brow**nn**

Angels are

beside you every step of the way.

They always have been, and they always will be.

Respecting the Journey

Eleanor Brown**nn**

Despite the blessings and the challenges, the hills and the valleys, the joys and the sorrows, the triumphs and the disappointments, the wins and the losses . . .

you're still alive.

Thank God and keep going.
Hold your head up today and **make the most of your circumstances,** whatever they may be.

Respecting the Journey

Eleanor Brownn

If you compare yourself to others, you'll always come up short.

That's because you're on a unique journey, unfolding in its own beautiful way.

Respecting the Journey

Eleanor Brow**nn** 💬

There were so many times along the way when you could have given up.

But you didn't.

Respecting the Journey

Eleanor Brow**nn**

When you trust your heart and stay on your path, miracles can happen.

Eleanor Brown**nn**

No fear.

Only peace.

Angels

surround

you.

Respecting the Journey

Eleanor Brow**nn**

There are times when you must walk away for your own survival.

Eleanor Brow**nn**

Your own fear
is the greatest
obstacle you will
face on your journey.

Let your

faith be bigger

than your fear.

Respecting the Journey

Eleanor Brownn

Put one foot in front of the other, no matter what. Enjoy the hilltop views, have courage in the valleys, pay attention to the bends in the road, cry when you have to, laugh when you can, be helpful to others, share your joys as well as your sorrows, and remember that God created you for a purpose.

Eleanor Brow**nn**

Change is hard.

Resisting change, harder.

Respecting the Journey

Eleanor Brow**nn**

You could have walked down a smoother road.

But you knew in your heart it was better to do what was right than to do what was easy.

Eleanor Brow**nn**

It's okay
to change
your mind.

Life is a series
of new
beginnings.

Respecting the Journey

Eleanor Brow**nn**

Your Life:

It's not a race —
it's a journey.

Respecting the Journey

Eleanor Brown**nn**

There were moments when it hurt so bad you couldn't breathe, yet somehow you survived the pain.

There were days when you could barely put one foot in front of the other, yet somehow you arrived at your destination.

There were nights when you cried yourself to sleep, yet somehow you held on until the morning.

Your life is nothing less than a miracle.

Respecting the Journey

Eleanor Brown**nn**

Refuse to become discouraged.

Draw upon the deep well of faith within you.

Look how far you have come.

Eleanor Brownn

Never tell yourself that you have wasted your time. No matter what you are doing – whether alone or with others, whether running or standing still, whether ideal or imperfect, whether at home or afar – you are learning, you are contributing, and you are growing.

Trust God and keep doing your best, because there never has been, and there never will be, a wasted moment in your life.

Respecting the Journey

Eleanor Brow**nn**

On some days,

one step closer

is enough.

Lifelong Learning

Eleanor Brow**nn**

You only have one life to live.

Make sure it's yours.

Lifelong Learning

Eleanor Brow**nn**

*E*very age
and every stage
of life has its
own possibilities.

Lifelong Learning

Eleanor Brownn

Never underestimate your ability to change.

You're not the same person you were even one second ago.

Eleanor Brownn

You're starting to see that what you feared was the end is turning out to be yet another new and wonderful beginning.

Eleanor Brown**nn**

Life is short.

Jingle your

bells.

Eleanor Brow**nn**

There is a gift only time can bring, and a story only the heart can tell.

Eleanor Brow**nn**

Never take life for granted.

Savor every sunrise, because no one is promised tomorrow . . .

or even **the rest of today.**

Eleanor Brow**nn**

No matter what **age** you are,

you're still learning,

you're still growing,

you're still changing.

Lifelong Learning

Eleanor Brownn

Time is a teacher.

The older you get,
the more you come
to appreciate
the wonder,
fragility, and
tenderness of life.

Lifelong Learning

Eleanor Brown**nn**

The **perfect age** for you to begin is whatever age you are **right now.**

Lifelong Learning

Eleanor Brownn

There will never be enough time to say all the things your heart meant to say.

Eleanor Brow**nn**

An **old person** knows what it's like to be young,

but a **young person** doesn't know what it's like to be old.

There's no substitute for life experience.

Lifelong Learning

Eleanor Brow**nn**

You were born with a blueprint inside of you.

The acorn has everything it needs to become an oak tree, but it can only express itself if it gets proper water and sunlight.

Surround yourself with people and ideas that nurture you and support you in reaching your full potential.

Eleanor Brow**nn**

Your vision is becoming clearer with time.

Eleanor Brown**nn**

One of the most
precious gifts of the
passage of time
is that it gives you
an ever-deepening
perspective on the
past, allowing your
understanding,
compassion,
and appreciation
to grow.

Lifelong Learning

Eleanor Brown**nn** 💬

Every age and every stage of life

has its own set of challenges
as well as opportunities.

You're not too old and
you're not too young
for goals and dreams.

Lifelong Learning

Eleanor Brown**nn**

Something inside of you was meant to blossom and grow.

Don't settle for anything less.

Lifelong Learning

Eleanor Brow**nn**

Your whole life is ahead of you.

Lifelong Learning

Eleanor Brow**nn**

Embrace life,

no matter how

late the hour.

Eleanor Brow**nn**

You'd better make
friends with Time...

because sooner or later
it will catch up with you.

Eleanor Brow**nn**

Take a chance. It's not too late to explore a new path.

Eleanor Brownn 💬

You're making progress because it's impossible for you to go backwards or even remain the same.

Life is an accumulation of experiences.

Lifelong Learning

Eleanor Brownn

Someone can live forever
in your heart, even
though they may be
long gone from
this world.

Eleanor Brownn

Life is a winding road,

with opportunities and obstacles along the way. As long as you are on the road, you are growing.

It doesn't always feel that way. You might feel stuck or even feel like you're going backwards. But in the Land of the Living, life can only move forward.

Pay attention. Trust your journey.

Eleanor Brown**nn**

It's not too late.

Some of your very best memories haven't even happened yet.

Gratitude

Eleanor Brow**nn**

Your darkest moments can provide the greatest light, if you use them to reflect upon and value what's truly important to you.

Gratitude

Eleanor Brown**n**

May you see your world in a whole new light.

May you see it through a lens of health, wholeness, and harmony.

Gratitude

Eleanor Brownn

Enjoy life.

You made it
through the
storm for
a reason.

Gratitude

Eleanor Brow**nn**

Don't miss all of **the**

good stuff that happens

today, because you're

thinking about all of **the**

bad stuff that happened

yesterday.

Gratitude

Eleanor Brown**nn**

Every sunrise is a gift.

Receive it with a grateful heart.

Gratitude

Eleanor Brow**nn**

Don't beg for crumbs

when a feast has already

been placed upon your table.

Gratitude

Eleanor Brow**nn**

Circumstances sometimes force you out of a situation.

You only realize later that you had already outgrown it.

Gratitude

Eleanor Brow**nn**

Be open to the possibility of an extraordinarily spectacular day.

Gratitude

Eleanor Brow**nn**

Be a blessing
to someone.

Your love can make
the difference.

Gratitude

Eleanor Brow**nn**

A grateful
heart
changes
everything.

Gratitude

Eleanor Brow**nn**

Remember to count your blessings, even when you have to count them through your tears.

Gratitude

Eleanor Brow**nn**

I hope something wonderful happens for you today.

Gratitude

Eleanor Brown**nn**

S ometimes a prayer gets answered that you didn't even know you were praying.

Gratitude

Eleanor Brown**n** 😊

Eleanor's Story Behind Writing the Poem "The *Other* Serenity Prayer"

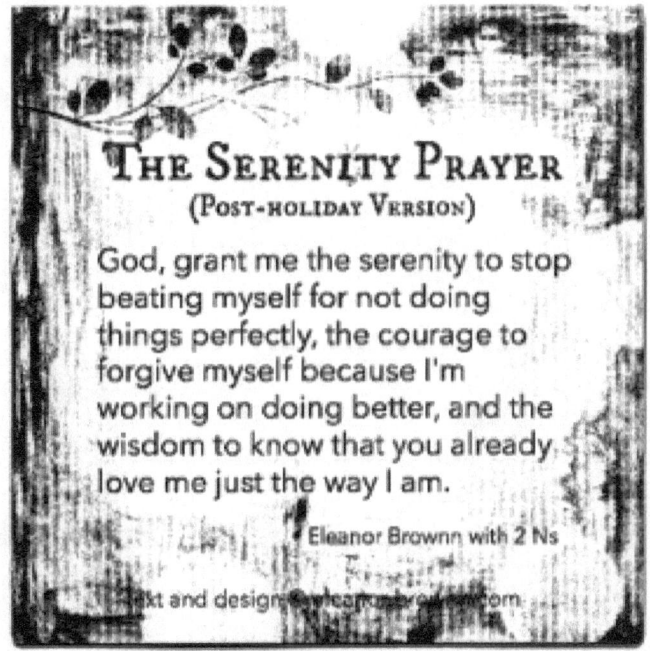

(The post: https://tinyurl.com/theotherserenityprayer)

Composed December 28, 2015, the original title of the poem was "The Serenity Prayer: Post-Holiday Version." I had a bad case of holiday blues after spending Thanksgiving and Christmas alone. At that point on the

Eleanor Brownn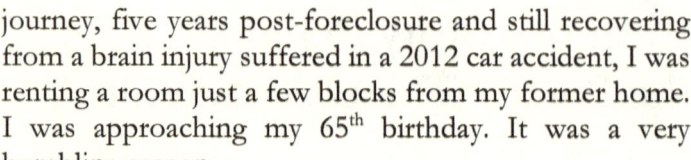

journey, five years post-foreclosure and still recovering from a brain injury suffered in a 2012 car accident, I was renting a room just a few blocks from my former home. I was approaching my 65th birthday. It was a very humbling season.

I was feeling ashamed and beating myself up about my situation. When I stared into the mirror I wondered how I could be so foolish to be where I was in life at my age. I had no one else to blame. A new year loomed ahead without much promise that things would change for the better. I got on my knees to say the traditional Serenity Prayer and found myself changing the words to match the despair I was feeling. But it ended in faith: *you already love me just the way I am.* I felt very much as if something had come through me.

When I created the meme for Facebook in December 2015, naming it the Post-Holiday Version of the Serenity Prayer, I didn't notice that I had made a typo on it – ironic since the poem is about perfectionism (the phrase should have read "beating myself *up*," not "beating myself"). The prayer got an overwhelming response from thousands of people who identified. Using the same text with the unrecognized typo, I renamed it "The *Other* Serenity Prayer" and reposted it in early 2016. It went viral. Then someone reposted the meme (typo and all) with my name cut off the bottom. The cropped version started popping up everywhere on various sites as a repost, followed by recreations with the author listed as "unknown" or with no citation at all. For someone who was finally finding her voice after 65 years, I didn't

Eleanor Brownn 🖤

take it well. I felt erased. But the genie was out of the bottle; a flood of knockoffs was out there without attribution.

I still have to take a few calming breaths whenever I see The *Other* Serenity Prayer online without my name. *God, grant me the serenity to stop myself from wanting to beat somebody up*.... The words to the poem came out of such a painful set of experiences that I feel a possessiveness about them. But the traditional Serenity Prayer, attributed to Reinhold Niebuhr, has had numerous variations created by different writers over time. Perhaps this is just some sort of spiritual exercise for me in letting go. I even manage to laugh at my reaction sometimes.

My perfectionism is imperfectly slipping away, slowly but surely, one day at a time.

Eleanor Brow**nn**

Other Publications
by Eleanor Brownn

Eleanor Brownn with 2N's
Inner self-compassion mindset brand. Eleanor's daily
writing and artwork on social media.
Facebook.com/BrownnCares/
Instagram.com/BrownnCares/

Be-Kinder-to-Yourself Store
Online shopping with print-on-demand merchandise
featuring Eleanor Brownn's self-compassion slogans.
https://tinyurl.com/ebrownn

*My Spiritual Sabbatical: What I'm Learning About Life After
Losing (What I Thought Was) Everything*
Personal blog. Chronicled in real time Eleanor's
adventures seeking to live life to the fullest between ages
60-70. EleanorBrownn.wordpress.com/about/

Your Whole Life is Ahead of You
Booklet of Eleanor's soul-baring essays and heartfelt
affirmations about growing older, making sense of the
past, and second chances, selected from her blog *My
Spiritual Sabbatical*. Heart Based Media; Los Angeles,
California (2018). Available on heartbasedmedia.com.

Eleanor Brow**nn**

MILE 9: The True Story of a Lifelong Couch Potato Who One Day Made a Decision That Changed Everything
Pushing age 50 and carrying an extra 80 pounds, Eleanor discovers an inner strength she didn't realize she had in this inspirational memoir of her journey to the Finish Line of the 1998 Los Angeles Marathon. Whatever goal you may be striving to achieve in your own life, have faith and keep moving forward . . . step by step. Bookmark Publications; New York, New York (2009). Available on Amazon.com.

Eleanor Brow**nn**

Contact the Author

Eleanor Brownn
Author | Speaker | Consultant
Contact: ebrow**nn**.com

Eleanor Brownn's mission is to inspire people to live a full life with self-compassion. Her words have encouraged millions of people around the world to be kinder to themselves, and she has a 30-year track record helping people live longer and healthier lives. Her own journey of the heart underpins what she offers in helping others break free from perfectionism.

As a personal growth consultant, she takes a holistic approach to providing life planning services and mentoring to support women as they go through life, career, and health challenges. Her work is rooted in a belief that positive change is possible at any stage of life.

As a thought leader, she is a writer and public speaker on the importance of positive self-talk who is frequently cited in a broad range of books, textbooks, professional training curricula, and articles related to compassion-fatigue and self-neglect among health and human services providers.

She holds a Master of Arts degree in Behavioral Science and is a Registered Life Planner®. Based in Los Angeles, California, Ms. Brownn consults virtually and face-to-face for individuals as well as organizations.